WHO WAS THE RED BARON?

Biography for Kids 9-12
Children's Biography Book

Speedy Publishing LLC
40 E. Main St. #1156
Newark, DE 19711
www.speedypublishing.com

In this book, we're going to talk about the Red Baron, who was a World War I flying ace. So, let's get right to it!

The first planes had only been flying for about ten years when World War I broke out in 1914. At the beginning, planes were used for gathering enemy intelligence and for dropping bombs, but then, fighter pilots began to shoot down enemy planes using rifles.

monoplanes dropping bombs

dogfight

To make the fighting more efficient, machine guns were mounted on planes and the era of aerial dogfights began. They called them "dogfights" because they were close range fights to the death. Many of the World War I fighter pilots who fought in dogfights became famous. They were called "aces" for their advanced skills as killers in the skies.

WHO WAS THE RED BARON?

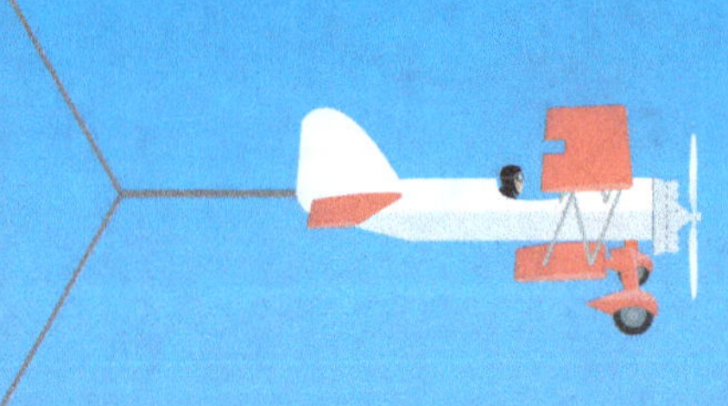

The pilot who shot down the most planes and became legendary in his own time was the Red Baron, whose real-life name was Manfred von Richthofen. He was a German who fought for the Central Powers, who were enemies of the United States and the Allied Powers.

Manfred von Richthofen

The Red Baron

He was called the Red Baron because he flew a bright red plane that was clearly visible in the sky. He was a disciplined, prideful, patriotic German with supreme hunting skills. He was a formidable enemy.

EARLY LIFE

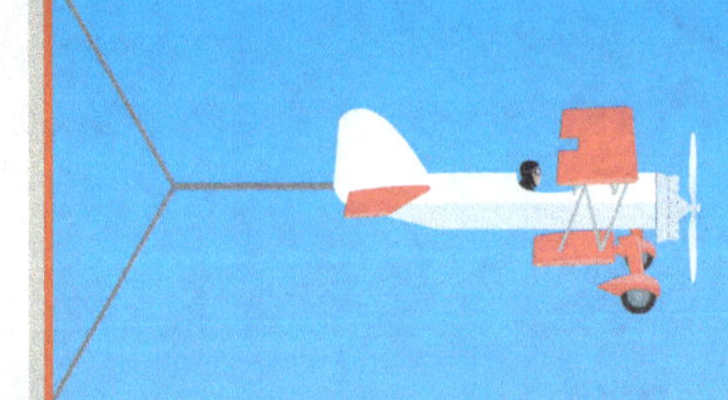

Manfred was born in 1892 to a noble family of Prussians who owned land. He grew up in Silesia, which is a part of modern-day Poland. His father, a career officer, and his mother's relatives, taught him how to hunt at a very early age.

E. OF BRANDENBURG
Mittelmark
POLAND
Spandau
Berlin
Küstrin
Kölln
Potsdam
Köpenick
Frankfort
Schwiebus
Züllichau
Krossen
Jüterbog
Wittenberg
Lübben
LOWER LUSATIA
Guben
Grünberg
Kottbus
Glogau
Sagan
Düben
Torgau
P. OF WOHLAU
Steinau
Wohlau
Wartenberg
Breitenfeld
Leipzig
OF SAXONY
UPPER LUSATIA
P. OF LIEGNITZ
Liegnitz
Öls
D. OF SILESIA
Grimma
Bautzen
Gorlitz
Goldberg
Breslau
Kötzschenbroda
Meissen
Dresden
Lobau
Rochlitz
Friedland
Schweidnitz
P. OF BRIEG
Freiberg
Pirna
Zittau
Hirschberg
Konigstein
Chemnitz
Oppeln
Tetschen
Klostergrab
Aussig
Braunau
Beuthen
Zwickau
Ossegg
Leitmeritz
Waldstein
Hermanitz
Neisse
Glatz
Kosel
Gitschin
Bunzlau
Joarhimsthal
Kaaden
Ratibor
Brandeis
Jagerndorf
Prague
Oderberg
Eger
Kolin
Friedland
Troppau
KINGDOM OF BOHEMIA
Teschen
Mies
Pilsen
Jankau
Olmutz
Leipnik
M. OF MORAVIA
Tabor
Klattau
Iglau
Kremsier
Brunn
Cham
Furth
Netolitz
Budweis
Znaim
Nikolsburg
Horn
Laa
ARCHDUCHY OF AUSTRIA
Krems
Korneuburg
Tulln
Eferding
Linz
Vienna

Silesia

RED BARON
RED
BARON

He and his two brothers hunted game in their private game forests. He loved hunting and would shoot down wild boar and deer. He was proud to display his kills on the walls of the family's castle. Later, he would bring this same drive to his aerial battles as an ace flyer.

At the age of 11, he became a student in the cadet corps of Prussia. He was bored by his studies, but when he joined the Uhlan First Regiment at the age of 19 he relished the opportunity to ride horses and be part of the cavalry. He fought briefly at the Russian front, but then his regiment was transferred to the West, where they didn't see much action.

Uhlan Regiment of Polish Army

Baron Manfred von Richthofen

Tired of being tasked with collecting cheese and eggs, he was dissatisfied that he wasn't fighting. He requested a transfer to a unit that was flying so he could participate in the battle. His request was granted in 1915.

FINALLY FLYING

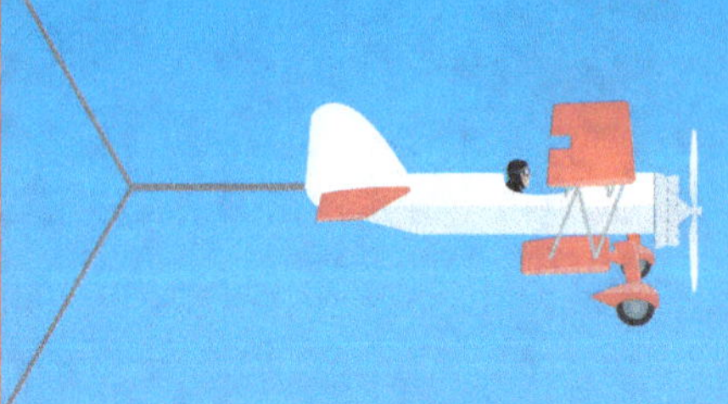

Back in the East, at first he was flying to gather intelligence on the enemy and then he was bombing. During the summer of 1915, he was flying with the 69th Flying Squadron. He didn't have a specialized expertise, so he was given the task of gathering intelligence regarding the enemy, just as he had when he was in the cavalry.

Manfred von Richthofen

2 Red Barons

Although he enjoyed the almost daily flights, he was still dissatisfied with his role and complained to his superiors. He was then transferred to a higher-level role, accompanying pilot Lieutenant Zeumer as they flew over the North Sea. He was an observer and gunner in the backseat. They once spotted a submarine, but didn't release bombs on it because they weren't sure which side it was on.

The very first English airplane he spotted was on the 15th of September 1915, but this encounter ended with not much damage to either plane. Zeumer and Richthofen both thought they could have done a better job with this opportunity for combat.

The red Fokker Dr1 of Manfred von Richthofen

Farman MF.11, WW1

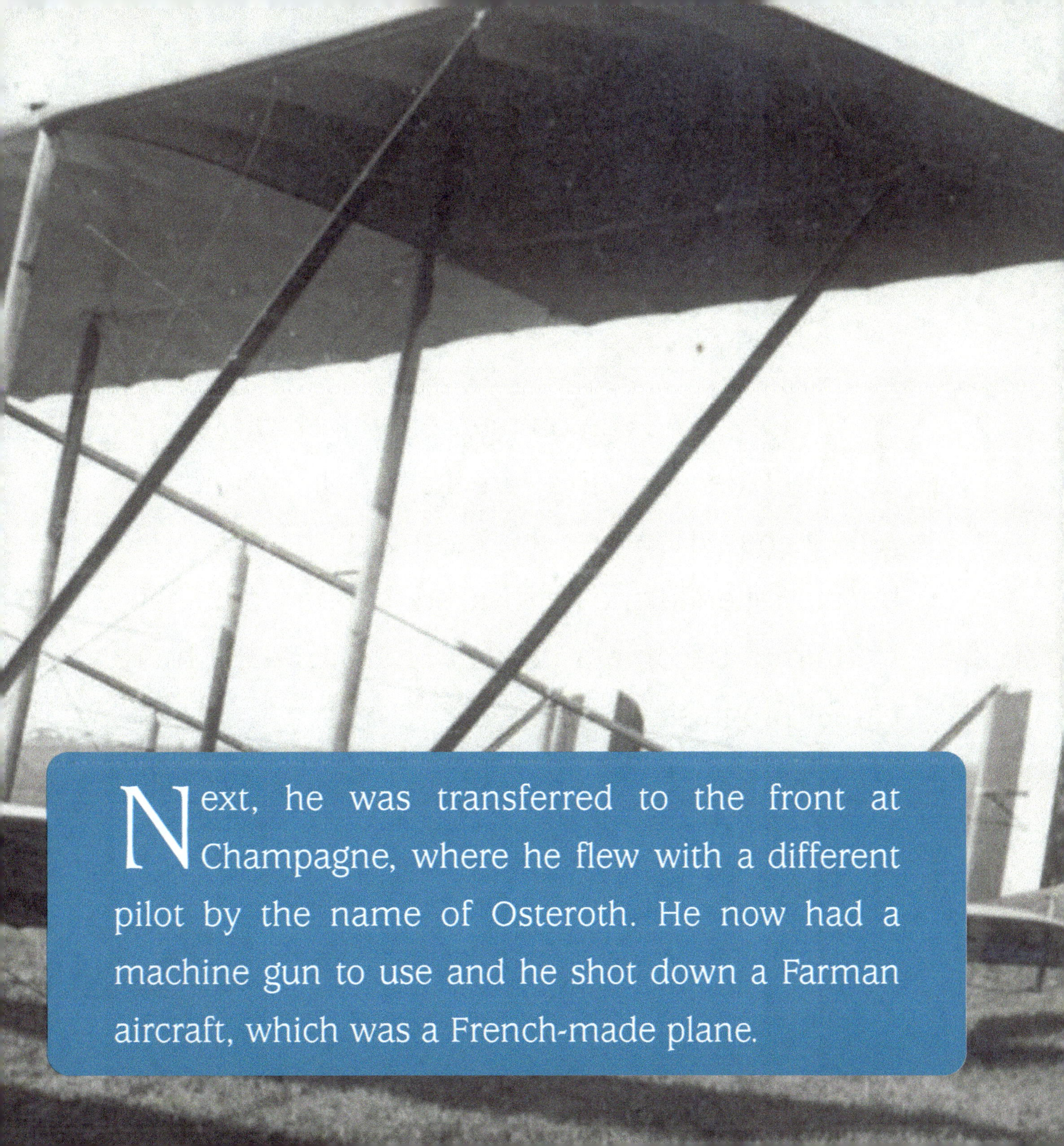

Next, he was transferred to the front at Champagne, where he flew with a different pilot by the name of Osteroth. He now had a machine gun to use and he shot down a Farman aircraft, which was a French-made plane.

However, he couldn't get official credit for this kill because the wreckage fell behind the Allied lines. However, his taste for the hunt had been awakened and he realized that he would have to train to become a pilot in order to make more career progress.

Manfred von Richthofen in front of his fighter squadron

Manfred von Richthofen inspecting a Fokker Dr.I triplane

He began pilot training in October of 1915. On his first solo flight he damaged the plane when he landed and had to continue his training. On Christmas Day, he finally aced his examination and was now qualified to fly at the age of 23.

In the spring of 1916, he joined his first air combat unit, KampfGeswchader 2, before the battle of Verdun. During this time, he learned how to handle an airplane that was a two-seater. He was assigned a reconnaissance plane. It was an Albatros BII, which had a maximum speed of only 66 miles per hour and a one hundred horsepower engine. It could only climb to a ceiling of about 10,000 feet.

Albatros BII

Fort Douaumont

Manfred set up a machine gun on the plane's upper wing. Piloting his plane over Verdun in April of 1916, he spied a French Nieuport plane. He opened fire on the pilot at a close range of 60 yards. The damaged plane dove into Fort

Douaumont, which was one of the many French forts surrounding the city of Verdun. Richthofen had his first sky victory, although he didn't gain any official credit for doing so since witnesses must observe the wreckage for the kill to be official.

In August of 1916, he had a chance meeting with the flying ace Oswald Boelcke, who had shot down about 40 enemy planes. He was looking for recruits for his new air command Jagdstaffel called Jasta 2 for short. He took a liking to Richthofen and after a quick interview took him along to the Somme, where one of the major battles of the war had started.

Oswald Boelcke

Battle of the Somme

BOELCKE'S PUPIL

Manfred was finally getting into the battle action that he had desired. He was learning quickly from his mentor Oswald Boelcke. During the bloody Battle of the Somme, they were fighting against the well-trained British air command.

On the 17th of September 1916, Boelcke was leading his men when they spotted the English planes, which were FE-2 two-seaters. The English planes were in a vulnerable position. They were flying toward the region of Cambrai with the Jasta 2 squadron positioned between them and the Allied lines.

FE 2b two seater biplane

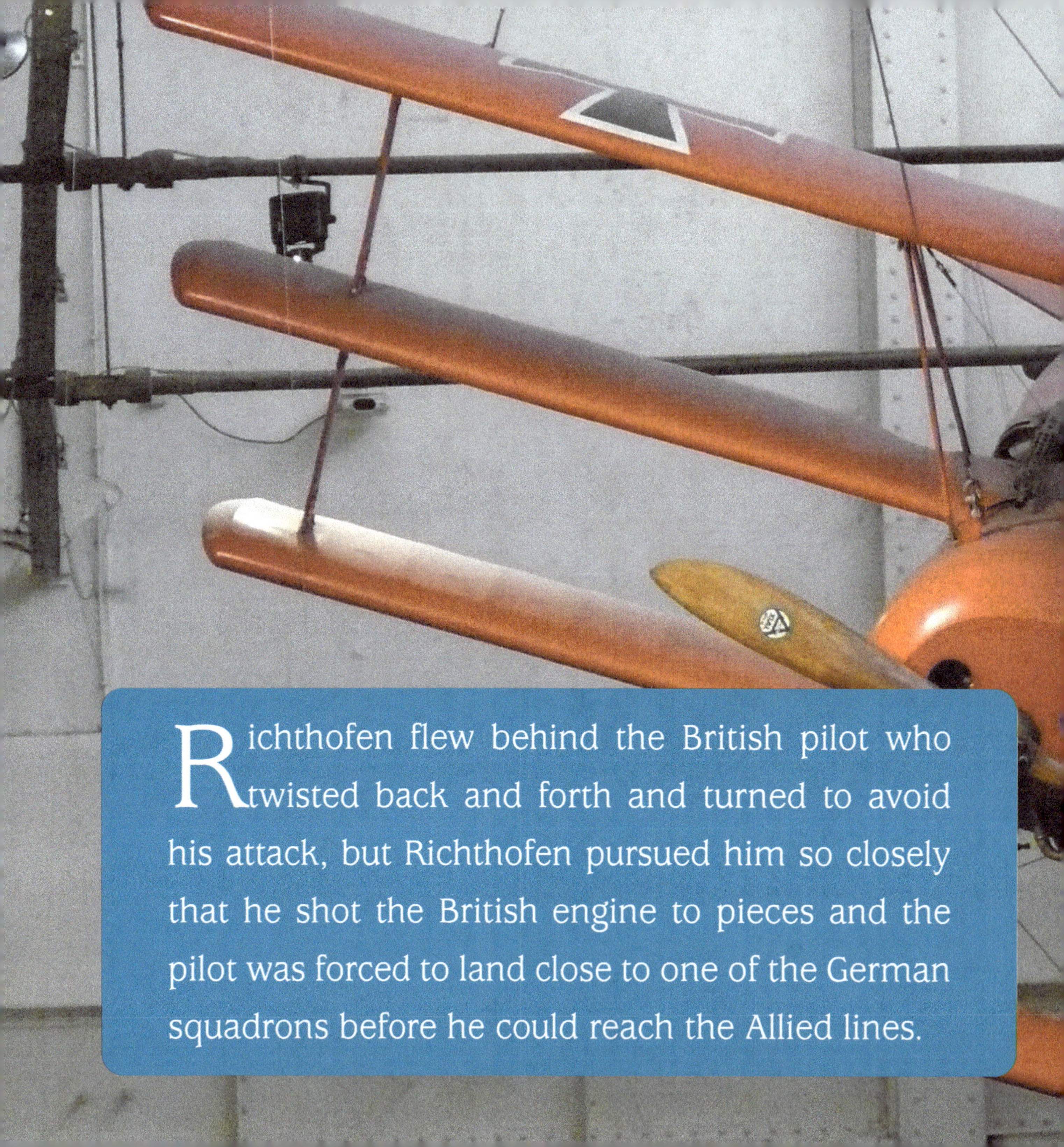

Richthofen flew behind the British pilot who twisted back and forth and turned to avoid his attack, but Richthofen pursued him so closely that he shot the British engine to pieces and the pilot was forced to land close to one of the German squadrons before he could reach the Allied lines.

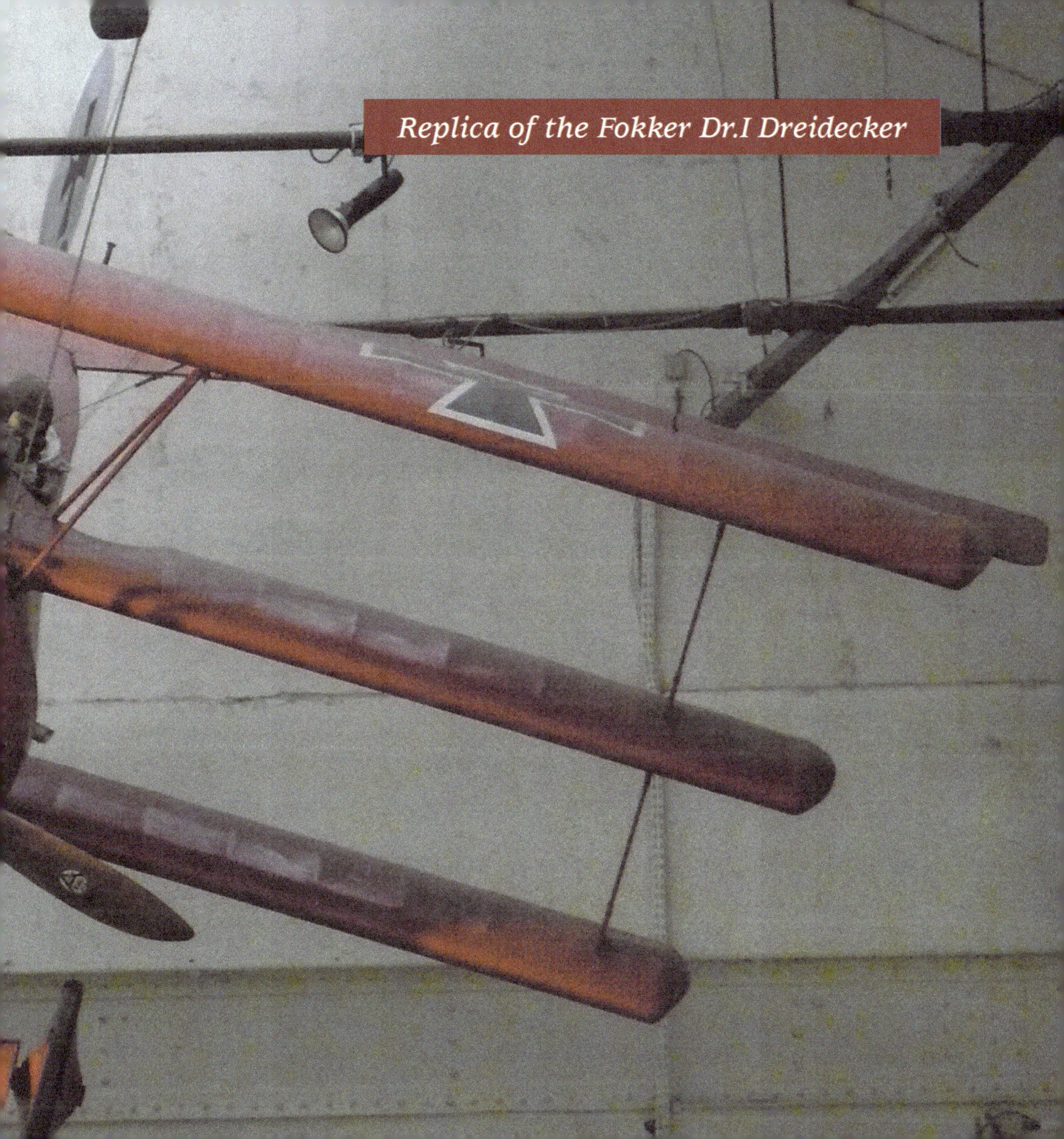

Replica of the Fokker Dr.I Dreidecker

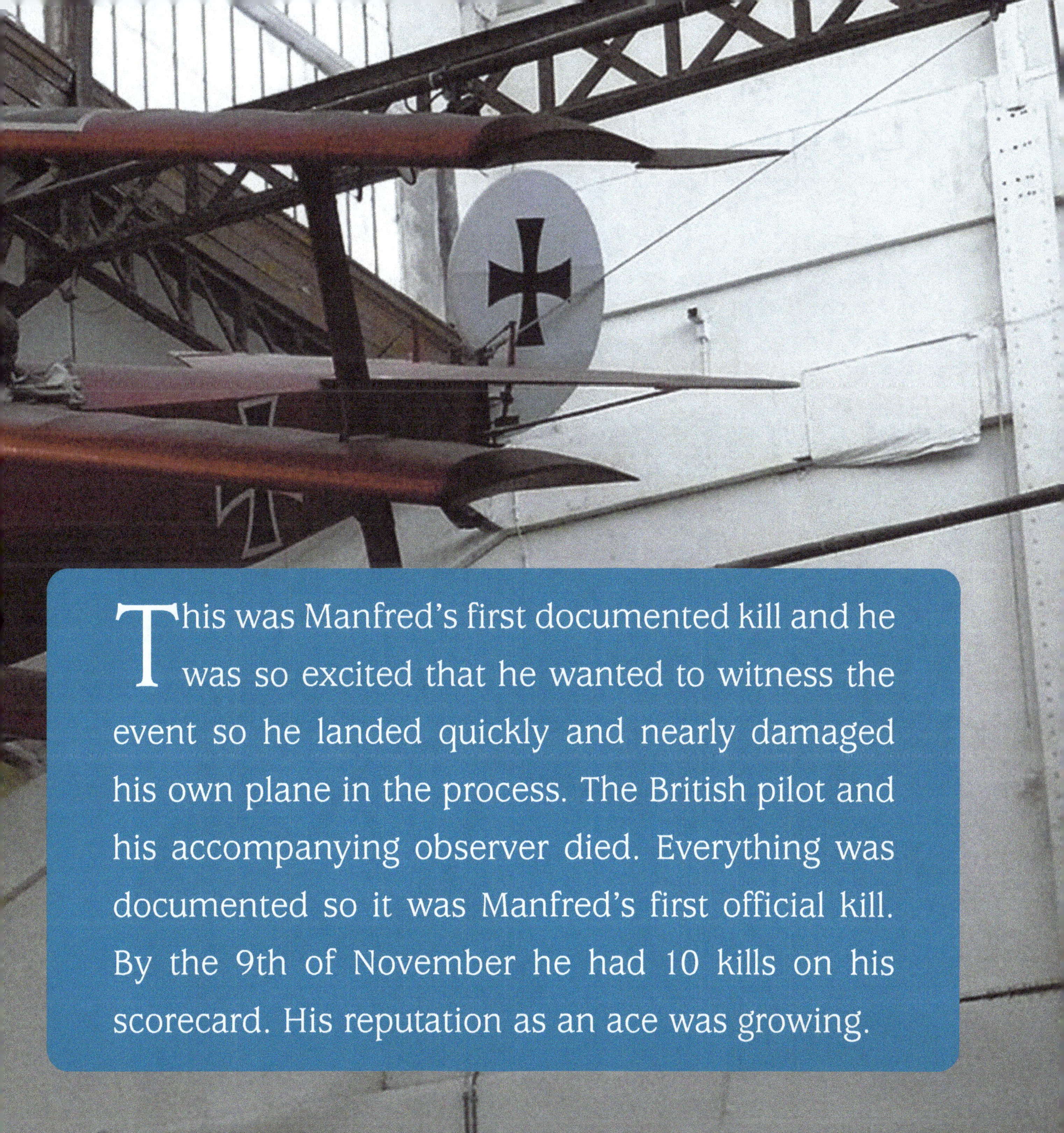

This was Manfred's first documented kill and he was so excited that he wanted to witness the event so he landed quickly and nearly damaged his own plane in the process. The British pilot and his accompanying observer died. Everything was documented so it was Manfred's first official kill. By the 9th of November he had 10 kills on his scorecard. His reputation as an ace was growing.

Fokker Dr.I

THE DEATH OF MAJOR HAWKER, V.C.

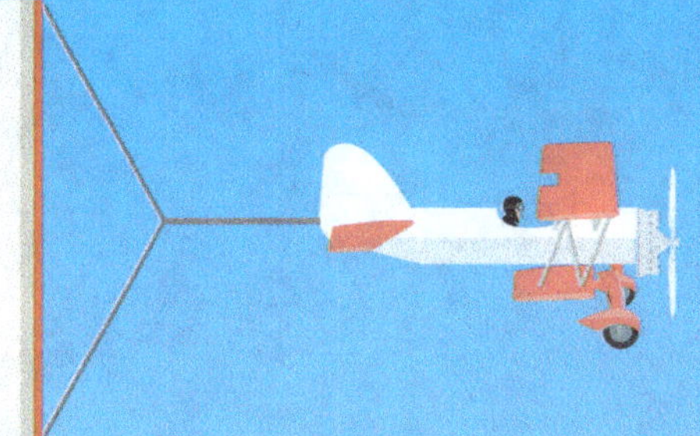

By this time, Richthofen thought of himself as a "big game hunter" and he wanted to kill the most important game. In November 23rd of 1916, he got into an aerial battle with Major Lanoe George Hawker, who had been called "the British Boelcke." He was the first fighter pilot to have received the prestigious British award for bravery, the Victoria Cross and his motto was "attack everything."

Hawker was leading three planes as they attacked German two-seater aircraft. But, this turned out to be a planned ambush. As the German two-seaters flew out of range, Hawker's men were attacked by Richthofen and other top pilots of Jasta 2. Two of Hawker's lieutenants were hit, but managed to escape as Hawker stayed to battle it out.

Fokker Dr.I guns

Fokker Triplane

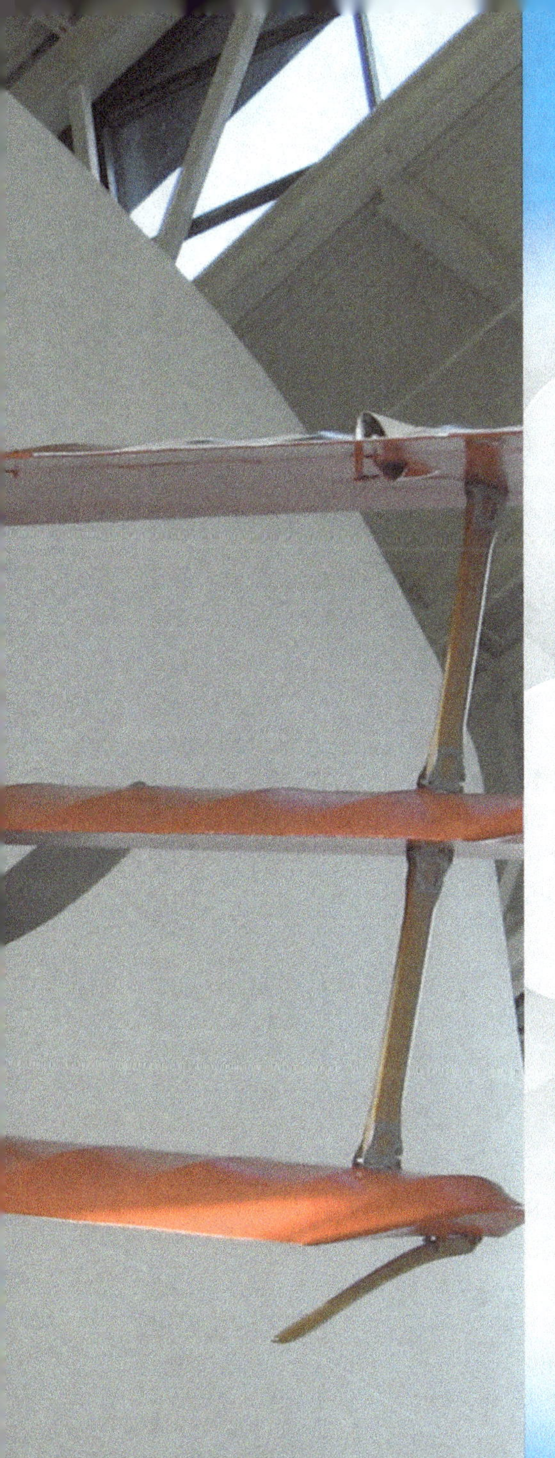

Hawker's aircraft and Richthofen's were now in a battle to the finish, beginning at 6,000 feet, twisting and turning up and down until at points they were only 50 yards above the ground. Richthofen continued with the machine gun fire and ultimately hit Hawker in the back of the head and killed him.

It was Richthofen's 11th kill and he had a tradition of ordering a silver cup that he had engraved with the aircraft and the victory's date. He also took Hawker's machine gun to decorate the door of his family's castle. Now that he had felled this "big game," Richthofen's reputation began to grow by leaps and bounds.

Red Baron

THE RED BARON

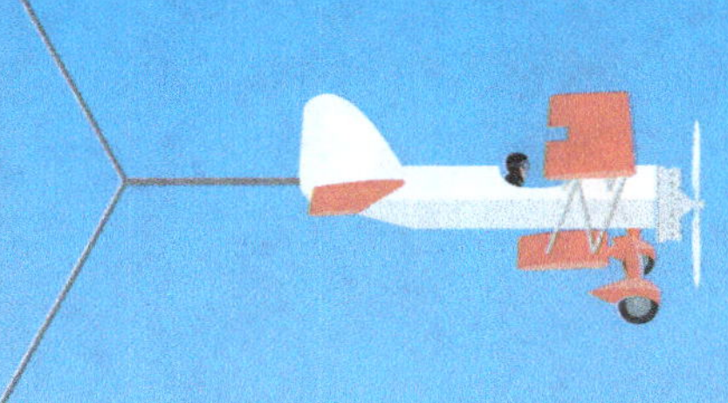

At the beginning of 1917, Manfred painted his plane with red paint. The British nicknamed him the "Red Baron." The Allied Powers wanted to shoot him down so that the Germans' morale would be shattered.

The Red Baron became commander of an elite team of German fighter pilots. They were named the Flying Circus due to their bright colors and the way they traveled from place to place like a traveling circus. The Red Baron had become legendary on both sides of the war.

HIER BEFAND SICH DAS GRAB
DES KÖNIGL. PREUß. RITTMEISTERS
U. JAGDFLIEGERS DES 1. WELTKRIEGES
MANFRED FRHR. VON RICHTHOFEN
„DER ROTE BARON"
1892 – 1918
1975 WURDEN SEINE STERBLICHEN
ÜBERRESTE AUF DEN SÜDFRIEDHOF
IN WIESBADEN ÜBERFÜHRT

SHOT DOWN

The Red Baron was finally shot down by a British fighter pilot on April 21, 1918. He was able to land his plane, but died soon after from the bullet wound. He was only twenty-five years of age when he died and had 80 kills to his name, more kills than any other pilot. The Allies buried him with full military honors.

Now you know more about the courageous and ruthless fighter pilot, the Red Baron. You can find more Biography books from Baby Professor by searching the website of your favorite book retailer.

Old Jerusalem

Visit
BABY PROFESSOR
EDUCATION KIDS
www.BabyProfessorBooks.com
to download Free Baby Professor eBooks
and view our catalog of new and exciting
Children's Books

www.ingramcontent.com/pod-product-compliance
Lightning Source LLC
LaVergne TN
LVHW082258150826
845677LV00009B/1651
* 9 7 9 8 8 6 9 4 3 4 1 1 1 *